T0171409

Evolving

New Attitude, New Direction, New Life In Christ Jesus

A Collection of Inspirational Poetry & Writings

Of

Doris M. Batson

iUniverse, Inc.
Bloomington

Evolving

New Attitude, New Direction, New Life In Christ Jesus

iUniverse books may be ordered through booksellers or by contacting:

iUniverse
1663 Liberty Drive
Bloomington, IN 47403
www.iuniverse.com
1-800-Authors (1-800-288-4677)

ISBN: 978-1-4620-1916-8 (sc)
ISBN: 978-1-4620-1917-5 (ebook)
ISBN: 978-1-4502-1598-5 (dj)

Printed in the United States of America

iUniverse rev. date: 5/18/2011

To

_____

From

_____

Date

_____

*"BUT GROW IN GRACE, AND IN THE KNOWLEDGE OF
OUR LORD AND SAVIOUR JESUS CHRIST."*
2 ND Peter 3:18 KJV

Dedication

෨෬

To my beloved Aunt, Geneva Berlina Collins, who was a dedicated servant, a woman of character and nobility, and truly a virtuous woman.

Thank you my Heavenly Father for pouring the words from my heart and giving me a spirit of inspiration. I love You and will forever give You all the Praise.

- Doris M. Batson

Acknowledgments

A heartfelt thanks to my parents, Rev. P.R. Moore, and Mrs. Jewetta C. Moore. What great parents you are! To my father; thank you for your determination, strength and continued vigilance that you inspire throughout the years; instilling the importance to always *"hold on to your faith,"* and to *"never give up on your dreams."* To my mother, Jewetta C. Moore; thank you for being a source of strength in helping me to realize, that whatever the situation, *"God is always in control,"* and He will make everything alright! Thanks for saying it over and over again. Your persistence and unwavering faith has really helped me to continue to grow in faith over the years. I love and admire you both for not only being such wonderful super role-models but also for your wisdom, dedication and love of the Lord. May God continue to bless.

To my daughter, Brittany De'Vonne Batson; thank you for being such a beautiful spirited and wonderful daughter. I appreciate so much your support and willingness to always take time to listen to my sometimes spontaneous thoughts of inspiration. I love you and encourage you to always aspire to your dreams, and continue to let God lead you.

I would also like to extend thanks to my co-workers: Fay Tacker; for the encouraging words and taking time to read and review my work on countless occasions, with patience and without reservation, and to Pam Slaughter; for all the overwhelming technological support, which has been invaluable, just to help me make it through the sometimes tenuous technological experience. I thank you both so much again. You are truly a blessing.

A special thanks to my church family, God's Will Missionary Baptist Church; Kasi Dinger; for the contribution of many of the beautiful art illustrations; and to a core of Christian friends,

Carolyn Westbrook, Tricia Billington, Alice Snow Mosley and my loving sister, Fay Taylor. I am appreciative to all of you for your support. You have been and continue to be a blessing in my life.

May God bless you all!

Table of Contents

Preface

The innocence of birth, the stages of growing, and the need of purposefully fulfilling one's life are all transitory stages relating to the process of evolving. These stages of life embrace the desire to enliven and nourish the very essence of our lives daily in helping to find our path and purpose in life.

The process of evolving can be a life changing experience. The inspiration of this book was derived from my own personal experiences in the search to find and understand purpose. As the journey and pursuit of purpose has led toward the encountering of many obstacles and dilemmas, I am still reminded that just as the caterpillar whose journey begins as an inconspicuously concealed life form; it later arises to emerge as an eloquent transformation. And in due season, if we allow the light of His love to indwell within, we too just as the emergence of the caterpillar, may grow to evolve, to come shining through with the eloquence of strength, grace and beauty.

The cycle of life as presented in *Evolving* is addressed in four stages: _Conception:_ the very essence of our core being; _Transition:_ letting go of our will to allow God's will; _Evolving:_ becoming renewed in the spirit and _Transformation:_ arising with affirmation of faith, renewed inner faith and spiritual empowerment.

Scriptural references and inspirational writings are also included and aligned with each poetic passage.

Preparing the way of acknowledging and becoming in touch with the presence of God, to find wisdom, inner strength and self-fulfillment, is the purpose and core message of "*Evolving.*"

But what is my purpose in life?

What has God planned for me?

Introduction

Embracing the Spirit Within

A Personal testimony

But what is my purpose in life?
   What has God planned for me?

These were questions that continually plagued my mind in search of finding a meaningful and purposeful life. I had always strongly believed there was a *"hidden dream and potential inside waiting to emerge"*---but understanding how to make it happen…that was the impending question.

Seeking continually for answers, I was drawn into the realm of listening to others who made the case of how to find a purposeful life: Their advice: "FIND WHEREIN LIES YOUR PASSION AND DO WHAT YOU ENJOY DOING THE MOST." The answer seemed very concrete and simple. Yet, why could I not know? I enjoyed doing many things; none of which were self-fulfilling. They were just not a passion for me.

As the journey toward the efforts to seek the discovery of purpose continued however, it led me to explore many paths. I found myself reeling from one thing to the other; senseless investments and many other countless venues. There was no clear vision, nor sense of direction.

"It seems as though I was operating in a state of emergency---wanting to make things happen right away, in the present time, instead of waiting patiently for God to allow things to happen in His own time."

The more I pressed forward…the more exhaustive the efforts. I was slowly and literally drifting more and more into my own thoughts and desires rather than focusing upon *"developing a closer relationship with God."* All of my efforts toward the pursuit of purpose continually left me in a quandary. There were many unanswered questions and still a feeling of emptiness left inside.

So here I was tired, exhausted, and drained. I had listened to all the advice. *"Still no direction."* I had done all I knew to possibly do. All the doors, it appeared were blocked and there was seemingly no way out.

"No matter how we may try to make a problem work or at times seek to find solutions or answers on our own---after a period of time…God has a way of allowing us to make a U turn, so to speak, which leads us right back to Him."

I found myself at a point in life where self-doubt began to invade my spirit. I began to wonder if in a sense, I would ever come to the realization of finding purpose.

"At a time, when it seemed, I was becoming most humbly submissive at the very least; God was strengthening and preparing me to become my very best."

As I persisted toward efforts to understand purpose, it would be oddly enough at a request made by my father that I would soon come to realize the meaning of fulfilling purpose.

At a celebration of my parent's 60th wedding anniversary, I recited a poem that I had written for the occasion entitled: *Beatitudes of a Christian Marriage.* My father who was in the process of preparing to write a book of a collected work of sermons and prayers, asked upon remembrance of hearing the reading of this poem, if I would consider writing inspirational poetry for his intended book.

"*Write Poetry?*" I thought the idea in itself was a little overwhelming. Remembering on several occasions when I did write poetry, it was always done on a whim---never really taken seriously. As I pondered the idea, I thought, "*What in the world could I do with poetry? What benefit could it possibly serve toward achieving my purpose and endeavors in life?*" Although questioning the idea, I ultimately agreed to collaborate in this venture; only with the intention of helping my father accomplish his dream. It would eventually become my own fulfilling purpose however, that would soon be realized.

"*No matter how we may try to accomplish things on our own, it has no merit. Our life, destiny and purpose are all in His hands.*"

As I continued contemplating on the idea of writing poetry, I found myself beginning to question and grapple with thoughts of "*What could I write? What could I say?*" Then, with only a pen in hand and a sincere desire, I sat quietly and began to prayerfully ask God for guidance.

"*Let it go...Let it happen with God. Embrace the light and spirit within.*"

Suddenly, as I began to write, it was as though my fears and doubts subsided. The words, the expression and the soul searching all began to just flow. Overcome with thankfulness, I realized that the gift being revealed was the inspiration of poetry. "*The true spirit and purpose had been there all along...right there within.*"

In all honesty now as I look back, the focus of my attention had always been centered upon *looking to see the bigger picture.* It seems so simple now...simple in realizing how within the daily routine and complexities of life, in efforts to find purpose, one may tend to overlook the *true inspirational spirit that dwells within.*

It is our charge to acknowledge God and to seek Him first. *As Proverbs 3:5-6 states: "Trust in the LORD with all your heart, and lean not to your own understanding; in all your ways acknowledge Him and He shall direct your paths."* If we keep the faith and allow God to become the center and focal point of our lives, He will in turn direct our lives toward finding a self-fulfilling and purposeful life.

"Wherein lies your passion"...a statement that would come full circle. God has designed each of us to fulfill purpose according to His will. Finding purpose, as I became aware is about the willingness to take the reigns out of our hands and place them in God's hands, to allow Him to steer the way. It's about embracing the spirit that dwells within. *"It's truly about having the faith to let go and to let it happen with God."*

The door was now open...I had found a place I could embrace.

Embrace

You were there in the very beginning
You gave me a brand new life
You are the very essence of my being
You are the depths of my soul's delight

You give me strength and comfort
In the shelter of Your arms
You're always right there
Leading me, guiding me
From all danger, hurt and harm

I find in You complete love
All that I am is because of You
You are the joy of my strength
The hope in all I do

There is none like You
In all the earth
None like You
I Proclaim

For You are the
Song of the worshipers,
The light of the heavens,
The praise of the dancers,
The joy in the laughter
Even the stars, the sun and
The moon beam with fervor
Awakening at the mention
Of Your Holy Name...

Oh I love You because of who You are
No one can ever take Your place...

It is Your love that makes me happy,

It is Your love that I seek,

It is Your love that I adore,

It is Your love
That I Totally
Embrace

Psalm 61:4
I long to dwell in your tent forever and take refuge in the shelter of your wings.

Deuteronomy 6:5
Love the Lord your God with all your heart and with all your soul and with all your strength.

Isaiah 48:13
My own hand laid the foundations of the earth, and my right hand spread out the heavens; when I summon them, they all stand up together.

Isaiah 54:5-6
For your maker is your husband the LORD almighty is his name-the Holy One of Israel is your redeemer; he is called the God of all the earth.

Isaiah 41:13
For I am the LORD, your God, who takes hold of your right hand and says to you, Do not fear; I will help you.

Psalm 121:7
The LORD will keep you from all harm-he will watch over your life.

Psalm 119:76
May your unfailing love be my comfort, according to your promise to your servant.

Philippians 2:10-11
That at the name of Jesus every knee should bow, in heaven and on earth and under the earth, and every tongue confess that Jesus Christ is Lord, to the glory of God the Father.

Whisper

Begin Anew…Awaken the spirit
Be still, Be silent and listen

Empty the heavy load that
Weighs you down
Tear down the walls of pain,
Disappointment,
And suffering,
Tear them down
Open up your heart
And listen

Begin Anew…there are streams
And rivers of waters
Flowing from the healing
Fountain, awaiting to
Fill the shallow emptiness
That floods within

Be still, Be silent and listen
Embrace the spirit
A gentle moment
To hear a quiet thunder
A calm serene
A silent voice within

A silence of Joy
Within my soul

A silence of calm,
Like the sea billows roll

A silence that gives me hope
When all hope is gone

A silence…a gentle spirit that
Gives me strength to carry on

Be still, Be silent, Listen
Lay aside every weight
For God knows our every need
All of our trials we are going through

If we listen and abide in the spirit,
He will show us in our hearts
Just what to do

Like a gentle breeze that swiftly blows
Like a candle light that ever glows
Like the sun that rises with a light of hope

He is waiting, He is there
A true comforter and friend
He is waiting, He is there
A silent voice within

There is a power raging inside of me,
But the storms of life that I
Must go through will
Only subside

If I arise…awaken the spirit,
And listen to hear
A gentle whisper
Of assurance

Listen to the silent voice
That dwells
INSIDE!

Whisper

Psalm 29:3-4
The voice of the Lord is over the waters; the God of glory thunders,
the Lord thunders over the mighty waters. The voice of the Lord is
powerful; the voice of the Lord is majestic.

Psalm 4:4
In your anger do not sin; when you are on your beds, search your
hearts and be silent.

Job 26:14
And these are but the outer fringe of his works; how faint the whisper
we hear of him! Who then can understand the thunder of his power.

Lamentations 3:26
It is good to wait quietly for the salvation of the Lord.

John 10:3-4
The watchman opens the gate for him, and the sheep listen to his
voice. He calls his own sheep by name and leads them out. When
he has brought out all his own, he goes ahead of them, and his sheep
follow him because they know his voice. But they will never follow
a stranger; in fact, they will run away from him because they do not
recognize a stranger's voice.

Chapter One
Conception

You are the potter I am the clay,
shape me and mold me, have thine own way.

A Willing Vessel:
Take me, Shape me, I'm Yours

> *"And the Lord God formed man*
> *of the dust of the ground and*
> *breathed into his nostrils the*
> *breath of life; and man became a*
> *living soul."*
>
> Genesis 2:7

Imagine the scenario; a potter who takes a piece of clay, shapes it, and forms it to make the shape of a desired vessel. After creating its shape, the potter then holds it in his hands and proudly looks upon his creation. Upon admiring and holding his vessel however, to his dismay, it suddenly falls from his hands, shattering and breaking into many tiny fragmented pieces, yielding disappointing results for the potter.

As we journey on life's path, there may be times when we through our own initiative, try to create what we desire or imagine our life's plan and purpose to be. However, even with all the preparations, planning and careful consideration of our lives; without the acknowledgement of seeking God first, just as the scenario of the potter whose vessel proved futile and fragile in his hands, we too as vessels may also become weak. The efforts of our works prove useless, if we do not allow God, the Master Potter to guide and direct our lives.

We have the assurance of knowing however, that just as we may fall susceptible to unsuspecting trials and tribulations, God already knows what we are going through. His thoughtfulness is to *"take us, shape, shield and strengthen us,"* to in time find identity and a purposeful path. Only God can, when we are weak and fragile, take the broken and shattered pieces of our lives and with loving care, *solidly and purposefully* put us back together again.

We are the exclusive works of God the Master Potter, all beautifully formed and created. We are living vessels, all uniquely *Touched by the Potter's Hand.*

*"We are God's children…God's creation,
all Touched by the Potter's Hand."*

T OUCHED BY THE POTTER' S HAND

If we look around and see what God
has created...
everything from the earth to the seas
from the heavens all abound.

If we can embrace the empowering
presence of His spirit, and the
awakening of His beauty...we can
rejoice in the abundance of His
wonder, that dwells within us
and all around.

If when we look beyond from the
farthest perimeters of the
stratosphere to the
inner most chambers of our
mind, our body, and
our soul...

God is omnipresent...
He is there...
Everywhere...

His amazing grace has kept us.
His omnipotent spirit dwells within us.
His wondrous works are
Infinitely immeasurable
and abounding...

as far as the eye
can behold.

Living vessels are we,
ornate in beauty,
intricately designed,

measured, weighed
and shaped miraculously by
His Almighty Hands.

God, in His infinite wisdom
envisioned our being…
then God spoke, and
upon His command…

Living vessels,
Transcended,
and
suddenly
without haste…

Celestial bodies rang
out of the darkness
of the universe with fervor…
to proclaim their rightful
purpose and their place.

We are a generation…
a destination of life
as it was meant
to be.

Living vessels
shaped, formed,
touched
and created by the

Hands of
God almighty.

From the Sun,
the Moon, the Stars,
the Planets, and all the
Heavenly bodies of the
Universe…

He created it!
A Vessel.

From the birds, the raven,
the eagle, the dove
and all creatures above
that stretch their wings
so gracefully…

He created it!
A Vessel!

From every plant of the field,
every herb…
to the creatures below with
their eloquent splendor
and majestic dignity…

He created it!
He created it All!
A Vessel!

From the misty waters of the
bellowing sea,
to the lofty hills of the
palatial mountaintops,
to the desolate valleys below…

He created it!
A Vessel!

From the lightning that flash
to the mighty rushing winds,
and the bolstering thunder
that rolls…

From the signs of the seasons,
the years, the months and the days,
to the hours, to the minutes,
and every second of
every day to unfold…

He created it!
He created it All!
A Vessel!

Then from the dust of the earth
with all power in His hands…

He took a lump of clay,
shaped it, molded it,
and formed it into His own image…
then blew into its nostrils
the breath
of life,
to create a
living soul…
The creation of man.

There is an imprint cast upon
all God's creation…all living
things in heaven and earth…
all things that have breath
and exist therein, great
and small.

A divine imprint,
made special for each of us;
each one,
uniquely signed by God.

We are a generation, a destination
of life as it was meant to be…

Living vessels,
shaped and formed by the
compassionate and
All Powerful
Hands
of
God Almighty.

Oh creatures below of the earth,
the seas, and in the
Heavens above…

Shout in song,
rejoice in praise,
of the Lord
our Creator,

For He is our Sovereign God,
He is our King…
Let everything that has breath
Praise Him, Lift Him Up…
Give Him the glory and
give Him the Praise.

For Thou art the Potter,
and we are the clay…
His mighty works are great…
an awesome wonder
and will forever stand.

Born of His spirit,
from the Living depth
and breath of our soul…

We are God's creation,
God's children,
Living vessels…

All Touched,
By the Potter's Hand.

Proverbs 3:19-20
By wisdom the Lord laid the earth's foundations, by understanding he set the heavens in place; by his knowledge the deeps were divided and the clouds let drop the dew.

Ephesians 1:13
And you also were included in Christ when you heard the word of truth, the gospel of your salvation. Having believed you were marked in him with a seal, the promised Holy Spirit.

Psalm 139:13-16
For you created my inmost being; you knit me together in my mother's womb. I praise you because I am fearfully and wonderfully made; your works are wonderful, I know that full well. My frame was not hidden from you when I was made in the secret place. When I was woven together in the depths of the earth, your eyes saw my unformed body. All the days ordained for me were written in your book before one of them came to be.

Jeremiah 10:12
But God made the earth by his power; he founded the world by his wisdom and stretched out the heavens by his understanding.

Psalm 33:11
But the plans of the Lord stand firm forever, the purposes of his heart through all generations.

Isaiah 64:8
Yet, O Lord, you are our Father. We are the clay, you are the Potter; we are all the work of your hand.

Genesis 2:7

The Lord God formed the man from the dust of the ground and breathed into his nostrils the breath of life, and the man became a living being.

Isaiah 49:15-16

Can a mother forget the baby at her breast and have no compassion on the child she has borne? Though she may forget, I will not forget you! See, I have engraved you on the palms of my hands; your walls are ever before me.

A Willing Vessel...

- *God often takes the shattered and broken vessel to shape and make it into what He wants it to be.*
- *As it is with the emergence of the butterfly, in due season, if we allow the light of His love to dwell within us, we too may evolve and come shining through with strength, grace and beauty.*

Prayer

Oh Lord, we are but lowly vessels. We ask that you would touch, cleanse, restore and make us whole again, to become purposeful vessels of Your will. We ask and pray in Your Holy and Righteous Name.

Amen

Chapter Two

Transition

A yielding vine growing in the Spirit.

A Yielding Vine:
Growing in the Spirit and Wisdom
of Humility

1 Corinthians 8:2-3
"The man who thinks he knows something does
not yet know as he ought to know. But the man
who loves God is known by God."

After all, what is knowledge without wisdom?

Growing up memories that are still fresh on my mind are of times I can remember hearing those in the community, church and even my parents say in regard to their wisdom and advice was to always be mindful to: *"stand firm on your beliefs."* They would go on to say; *"remember; no matter how much educational wisdom you may gain, nothing can compare to the knowledge and importance of always seeking God first in all that you may aspire to do."*

With a presumption of knowledge as one may acquire it however, there may be at times a desire to challenge or impose the enlightenment of intelligence upon others. As this may occur, the action initially tends to overpower the whole understanding that *"knowledge in and of itself is of God, and can only be empowered and endowed by God."*

If we acknowledge and allow His Spirit to indwell within, we may embrace the *knowledge of inspired wisdom*, instinctively instilled within us. I reference this insight in terms of observing my mother throughout the years, watching closely how she continues to use wisdom instinctively inspired; referring to it many times as *"just using plain common sense."* I have found her definitely to be a *true warrior*, in the sense of how she respectfully understands the true meaning of how to aptly apply and speak the knowledge of wisdom. Toward any given situation, her philosophy is in essence, *"telling it plain and simple."* No *"sugar coating," with flamboyant language…no additives in trying to practically analyze or make adjustments in efforts to make it seem better or right, if it's not.* I admire her because it seems the book and knowledge of her insight, is really about applying the answers from another perspective, that *of life's experiences, and most importantly, of God whom she trust explicitly.*

In talking with my mother, like a sister and friend at times; so eloquently, she opens up her book of knowledge and began to candidly draw upon the experiences of her life stories. And just like a storyteller, she portrays the right experience to fit the problem or situation. Even though, I may hear the same stories which seem to be in replay sometimes, only with a different tune or version, still no matter how many times I hear them, they inspire me. I have come to realize, that her sense of wisdom is not about the idea of knowledge in the story itself, trying to allegedly display it like a trophy--*"it's really about the inner voice of wisdom, courage, meekness, beauty and strength shining through like a beacon of light from within."*

Paul in his appeal to the Corinthian church made aware exemplifying principle characteristics in his references of the fruits of the spirit. In Galatians 5:22-23, he listed them as, *"love, joy, peace, patience, kindness, goodness, faithfulness, gentleness and self-control."* As we seek to endear these principles, we can embrace in kind the *spirit of humility,* which is in a sense a virtue of meekness in itself.

To become free from self-absorption, we must strive to remove self-pride, remembering, *humility is realizing that without God we can do nothing.* Only God can enlighten our minds, and in time exalt us and give true wisdom and humility of the spirit. It is only then can we discard worldly wisdom, and grow to endear the spiritual wisdom of God.

The enlightening message, inspired of the poetic passage entitled: *Inconceivable;* is that, *"God is the source of understanding for all things in and of itself."*

The inquiry passage of *Inconceivable,* begins with an inquisitive young boy gazing upon the night sky, awestruck by what he sees. He inquires of his father many questions about the fascination of the universe. His father in turn begins to try and explain to his son his inability to explain the inexplicable.

"For my thoughts are not your thoughts, neither are your ways my ways, thus saith the Lord."

Isaiah 55:8

INCONCEIVABLE

The Inquiry...

"It is amazing to me Dad," a seven year old boy inquisitively said to his father, as he sat looking out his window. In a moment of contemplation, and continually gazing out into the night sky, he repeatedly stated in a perplexing voice...*"it is absolutely amazing!"*

As his father listened intently, he asked, *"what is it son, that has piqued your interest?"*

The little boy, seemingly still captivated and overwhelmed by such an extraordinary sight, and with his eyes still glaring from the brightness of the moonlight answered his father saying, *"there must be a billion, gazillion stars shining tonight... and it seems they are all beaming, sparkling and looking down on me!"*

As his father continued to see the curiousness in his son's eyes; he reflected back in time for a moment; remembering a conversation he had once with his own father. With anticipation, he beamed however; at the opportunity to convey a message to his son his father had once shared with him. He knew it would be a memorable message. One that he would soon never forget!

INCONCEIVABLE

The Message...

Son, how do I begin to tell you?
How can you understand?
As you look upon the universe,
The stars and the moon,
It is God's creation...
Undeniably
Incomprehensible...
The works of a miraculous
Master plan.

Son, how can I begin to tell you?
For there is no comprehension of it...
No man can understand it...
Only just behold
Its beauty,
Appreciate it...
Stand in awe of
His mighty works...
For it is more than enough
Just to revere the
Wondrous works of
His Almighty Hands.

It is
Inconceivable
To me...

How He created
The countless grains of sand...
The sun, moon, and the
Stars above...

How He fashioned and
Formed the universe,
The earth, its creatures,
And all the inhabitants thereof.

You see words cannot describe it...
One can only stand in awe of it...
And revere it...

I cannot comprehend it...
The perception of the beauty of
God's creation...
It is just an immense wonder...
So amazing to see.

No scientist,
Lawyer,
Or skilled physician
Can successfully analyze it...

No psychologist,
Astrologist,
Or noted acclaimed
Mathematician,
Can factually theorize it...

No calculative minded
Genius can even summarize or
Conclusively gravitate the

The immeasurable
Dynamics of it.

There is just No definitive scientific
Or equivocal explanation.

The scripture says:
"For if any man think he knoweth anything, he
Knoweth nothing yet as he ought to know."

For no one can implicitly derive
At a conclusion that can be understood.

"For My thoughts are not your thoughts,
Neither are your ways My ways, thus saith
The Lord."

So son, just remember,
As you absorb and behold
The beauty of
God's creation…
Be thankful of it, and
Stand in awe of it…

For God's work is to be
Revered and
Appreciated
Just, as it should.

There is none like the Lord…
He is the source
Of every breath we make.

There is none like the Lord…
For He is
God…
Our Father...

And He knows our actions,
Our words, our deeds
And every step we take.

So when you look up in the
Heavens and see the glory of
His Mighty works...

How it glows so fervently
With such an immense array...

All I can tell you Son, is to
Say, "thank you Lord,"
And glorify in it...

Because you see,
I cannot fathom it,
Indelibly define it,
Nor even comprehend it...

God's mighty works
Are beyond comprehension.
It is Inconceivable.

But I say to you...
Be mindful to know...
That all you need to know...
Is that God created it!!!
And that settles it!

Because God's work
Undeniably,
Speaks...
For itself!!!

Amos 4:13
He who forms the mountains, creates the wind, and reveals his thoughts to man, he who turns down to darkness, and treads the high places of the earth-the LORD God Almighty is his name.

Isaiah 55:8
For my thoughts are not your thoughts, neither are your ways my ways, declares the LORD.

1Corinthians 1:31
Therefore, as it is written: "Let him who boasts boast in the Lord."

Jeremiah 10:12
But God made the earth by his power; he founded the world by his wisdom and stretched out the heavens by his understanding.

Jeremiah 33:3
Call to me and I will answer you and tell you great and unsearchable things you do not know.

Proverbs 23:15
My son, if your heart is wise, then my heart will be glad.

Psalm 145:3
Great is the LORD and most worthy of praise; his greatness no one can fathom.

Ecclesiastes 5:7
Much dreaming and many words are meaningless. Therefore stand in awe of God.

Hebrews 11:2
By faith, we understand that the universe was formed at God's command, so that what is seen was not made out of what was visible.

"Oh Rejoice in the Lord, for my change is coming."

God's Precious Petal

As I think back on how life used to be
A tear begins to fall
Only to drop, beside the morning dew
Already settled on one of God's precious petals

The secret sound of that one teardrop
Is magnified ten thousand times in my head
And just adds to the confusion and frustrations
Already in place

As I lift my head, I look for that
One ray of hope that others speak of
Hoping that it will dry up the rivers I've cried
And the overflow of hurt
And pain in my heart

As I hold on to fond memories
And recollections of precious moments
I pray for change that one day I will
Be able to smile again
Trusting God, to help me trust
Myself
For my flesh gets weak

As I kneel before the presence of
God I'm thankful
But upon arising, I stumble because
The weight of my burden and sadness
Was not completely left there

As the day turns night and the night turns day
And the cycle of life makes another complete circle
I begin to think back on how life use to be

But this time, I don't hear the tear drop
Neither do I search for that ray of hope

But I suddenly realize that God's perfect
And precious petal
Is now in full blossom and it smells so
Beautiful and fresh
For the touch of a tear stimulated a spurt of
Growth to fulfill its destiny and position
On God's earth

Oh rejoice in the Lord for
My change is coming!

-Brittany D. Batson

Psalm 42:5
Put your hope in God, for I will yet praise him, my Savior and my God.

Job 22:27
You will pray to him, and he will hear you, and you will fulfill your vows.

John 16:24
Ask, and you will receive and your joy will be complete.

Isaiah 40:31
But those who hope in the LORD will renew their strength. They will soar on wings like eagles; they will run and not grow weary, they will walk and not faint.

Philippians 4:4
Rejoice in the LORD always. I will say it again, Rejoice!

1 Peter 1:6-7
In this you greatly rejoice, though now for a little while you may have had to suffer grief in all kinds of trials. These have come so that your faith of greater worth than gold, which perishes even though refined by fire may be proved genuine and may result in praise, glory and honor when Jesus Christ is revealed.

Everything in its season--in its time.

In its time

The Rain falls—
Mellowing down like
Sparkles of glittering ice

The soil refreshed
Dewdrops scatter
Accentuating the atmosphere
Like the fragrance
Of the morning light

Life emerges
Penetrating
Saturating
Expectation of new birth
Unearthing its best

Budding roots
Now rising –
Enlivening its way
Touching the grasp
Of intrigue
Excitingly

The flowers, blooms, the critters
Loom—
The grass and all within set free

Gathering, an array of beauty
Everything
Surging, prevailing
Unique in its kind

Everything in its season
Springing forth

Exuding new life-
New energy
Increasingly flourishing
In its moment and
In its time

Psalm 1:3
And he shall be like a tree planted by the rivers of water, that bringeth forth his fruit in his season; his leaf also shall not wither; and whatsoever he doeth shall prosper.

Ecclesiastes 3:11
He has made everything beautiful in its time.

Philippians 4:8
Finally, brethren, whatsoever things are true, whatsoever things are honest, whatsoever things are just, whatsoever things are pure, whatsoever things are lovely, whatsoever things are of good report; if there be any virtue, and if there be any praise, think on these things.

Romans 12:12
Be joyful in hope, patient in affliction, faithful in prayer.

2 Peter 3:18
But grow in the grace and knowledge of our Lord and Savior Jesus Christ.

Ezekiel 34:25
I will bless them and the places surrounding my hill. "I will send down showers in season; there will be showers of blessing.

Jeremiah 31:22
For the Lord hath created a new thing in the earth.

Lamentations 3:25
The LORD is good unto them that wait for him, to the soul that seeketh him.

God's Fruitful Garden

The seed awaits the awakening – the bloom of a bountiful harvest – an immense wonder – soon to be revealed – uprooted – arising to grow and grasp the spirited warmth and glow in the light of God's Fruitful garden.

There is a sense of renewal in the air – planted seeds – like radiant dew drops – now shimmering in the bask of the morning sun – each carefully guided by the light of His wisdom – compassionately planted purposefully – diligently – in place. Each now arising a gift of God's glory – flourishing vines emerging in time – to grow richly – multiply – increase in the beauty and spirit of His grace.

Many seeds planted and chosen for the spiritual harvest – growing in an abundance of Love - Joy- Peace - Patience - Kindness-Goodness -Faithfulness – Gentleness and Self-Control – Blessed seeds sown in the spirit – soon to be a delightful compassion for the soul.

Uprooting was LOVE – its roots gently lifting and surging toward the rising of the sun – beaming with a spirit of warmth and compassion – like the shine of a gentle rain. Then there was JOY – whose vines were soaring intently free – with an unshakeable spirit of thankfulness and gratefulness – in light of victories won and triumphs still yet to gain.

The spirited root of PEACE was lying still – its roots firmly planted solidly with hopeful anticipation and PATIENCE was rooted nearby awaiting to arise – yet remaining calm in its spirit – with graceful expectation.

The seeds of KINDNESS and GOODNESS were emerging – rising up from the earth with a light of thoughtfulness and tenderheartedness – each were mostly known for their heartfelt appeal. Then there were other seeds growing of FAITHFULNESS and GENTLENESS beaming strongly together – rising fluently in a spirit of humility –strength—and with a steadfast zeal.

Yet there was one more seed planted and growing in the spirited garden –its vines rising swiftly and vigorously to the light of the skies—one whose nature was immensely strong willed and bold. But in the midst of its determination to surge and rise so free – it suddenly remembered in its spirit to wait patiently – remain calm and composed at all times – always in SELF-CONTROL.

The fruits of the spirit—arising in many colors, many shapes, many hopes, dreams and aspirations—all waiting to shine--seeds once planted now growing in God's fruitful garden--beautifully in sight.

A harvest of abundance— saturated splendor--flourishing seeds--each purposefully planted to grow distinctly-- individually and uniquely—blessed seeds of the True Vine -- an immense portrait of beauty—God's intriguing wonder of delight.

1Peter 5:8
For this very reason, make every effort to add to your faith goodness; and to goodness, knowledge; and to knowledge, self-control; and to self-control, perseverance; and to perseverance, godliness, and to godliness, brotherly kindness; and to brotherly kindness, love. For if you possess these qualities in increasing measure, they will keep you from being ineffective and unproductive in your knowledge of our Lord Jesus Christ.

John 15:5
I am the vine, ye are the branches: He that abideth in me, and I in him, the same bringeth forth much fruit: for without me ye can do nothing.

Isaiah 43:18-19
Forget the former things; do not dwell on the past. See, I am doing a new thing! Now it springs up; do you perceive it?

Galatians 5:22
But the fruit of the spirit is love, joy, peace, patience, kindness, goodness, faithfulness, gentleness and self-control.

James 4:10
Humble yourselves before the Lord and he will lift you up.

Galatians 6:9
Let us not become weary in doing good, for at the proper time we will reap a harvest if we do not give up.

Psalm 60:21
Then will all your people be righteous and they will possess the land forever. They are the shoot I have planted, the work of my hands, for the display of my splendor.

Hosea 10:12
Sow for yourselves righteousness, reap the fruit of unfailing love, and break up your unplowed ground; for it is time to seek the LORD until he comes and showers righteousness on you.

A Yielding Vine...
- *Knowledge in and of itself is of God, and can only be empowered and endowed by God.*
- *Trust in God to trust yourself to find and endear the knowledge of spiritual wisdom.*
- *Grow in renewed strength to flourish in due season and in due time.*

Prayer

Oh Lord, we yield as submissively as we know how seeking Your loving spirit to indwell within. Where we need guidance and direction, please help us to
find our way. Enlighten our minds that we may speak with wisdom,
and let Your ever-present spirit touch our lives that we may continue to grow in grace. We ask and pray in Your Holy and Righteous Name.

Amen

Chapter Three

Evolving

*And we may grow to evolve and become
the beautiful creature God wants us to be.*

Changes:
A blessed creation in progress growing still

Galatians 6:9
"Let us not grow weary while
doing good, for in due season we
shall reap if we do not lose heart."

The infinite wonder and beauty of God's creation is prevalent and around us in so many ways. From the vibrant colors of flowers that bloom in the spring to the green grass that seasonally change. In all stages of life, *"life gives life,"* and evolves like the birth of the dawning of a new horizon. Everything that has life continues to evolve...ever growing, ever changing.

As Ecclesiastes 3:1 states, *"There is a time for everything."* Nothing remains the same. God allows us the potential and time to grow to experience change. However, the willingness to wait patiently for our change to come in due season, may at times become the unintentional imposition. And the questions may still prevail..."*what is my purpose, and when will my change come?"*

However, like a caterpillar that springs from its lifeless form to emerge as a beautiful and miraculous creature...in time, our change will come. And as we grow, we too may become the beautiful creature God desires us to be.

I am reminded of a situation once, when teaching a painting unit to my art students in class. I had asked them to paint the simple shape of an apple. They were also asked to observe very closely to see if they could find colors on the apple other than the color red. They looked at me as though to ask, *"why are you asking us to find other colors? The apple is red!"* As I saw their puzzled faces, I expressed to them that even though the apple may be perceived as being red; there are still many other colors that may be hidden. *"Look closely again,"* I asked. Their persistence continued however that the apple was undoubtedly red. Then suddenly, as they sat quietly observing; it was as though a light turned on in their inquisitive and curious minds. One little boy said, *"I think I see purple."* Another called out green, and so on. They had noticeably taken the time to really look and observe closely; and in doing so, found that what had been hidden before, was now quite obvious and evident right before their very eyes.

God has designed a plan and purpose for our lives. *He already knows the path of our intended purpose.* So many times as we become caught up in the daily routine and complexities of life, it may tend to lead us in ways of continually operating in the same usual manner. The potential to change to do things differently than ways we are accustomed, essentially becomes embedded within.

We are blessed by our creator with a mind to *explore, think and even imagine.* We must *release ourselves from the trap* that binds us, to *explore and imagine the possibilities.* If we allow ourselves to *"break the cycle,"* to see and do things differently, we may then potentially come to discover *hidden qualities, (a special uniqueness within us all),* and to experience change and purpose in time and in due season.

"A blessed creation in progress growing still."

Evolving

Evolution, a change
In Your Will
Am I
A new creature
Awaiting to emerge

Like the light of daybreak
Before dawn
In anticipation of the
Rising sun

Like a flowering vine
Submissively
Surging
Towards the sky

In Your Will
Am I
Evolving
In Your Will
Am I

Like an aromatic scent
Of a budding rose
Awaiting to shower
Its fragrance
So free

Like an empress vessel
Awaiting the gentle
Calm of a treacherous
Raging sea

Like a captive bird
Longing to spread its
Wings so free

I Evolve

To everything
There is a season
A time to plant
A time to grow
A time to uproot
that which is planted
A time to
reap the harvest sown

A planted seed
Now arises
With strength and beauty
All its own

On a mountaintop of
Possibilities

I Evolve

In light of
Impossibilities

I Evolve

Ever Growing
Ever Changing

I Evolve

Submissively, I yield
A blessed creation in progress
Growing still

With outstretched
Hands
Lifted up high

A towering vine
Reaching towards the sky

On the wings of Your Love
I Evolve

In Your Will
Am I
Evolving

Ever, growing
Ever changing

I Evolve
In Your Will
Am I

Psalm 16:6
The boundary lines have fallen for me in pleasant places; surely I have a delightful inheritance.

Isaiah 43:18-19
Forget the former things; do not dwell on the past. See, I am doing a new thing! Now it springs up; do you not perceive it?

Psalm 52:8
But I am like an olive tree flourishing in the house of God; I trust in God's unfailing love for ever and ever.

Matthew 5:16
In the same way, let your light shine before men, that they may see your good deeds and praise your Father in heaven.

Job 17:9
Nevertheless, the righteous will hold to their ways, and those with clean hands will grow stronger.

1 Corinthians 3:7
So neither he who plants nor he who waters is anything, but only God, who makes things grow.

Mirror, Mirror
True Reflections

How often is it that we may tend look at ourselves in the mirror; and as we look become so engrained in the perception of physical beauty that we do not impose to see a *true reflection of inner beauty?*

Truly this was a mindset that had been infused into my way of thinking during my growing up years. There was a phrase however, that became in these early years, an eye opener for me, which stated: *"Beauty is only skin deep."* This was a popular slogan that had caught on in the early seventies. The words were initially performed as a song, and the significance of its impact allowed a chance for me to look at myself uniquely and individually. It gave a feeling of realizing, it was okay to be different. In essence, it was okay to be me. Slowly, the image of what I had felt beauty was and what it represented became in actuality a facade.

Even though this phrase had significant meaning, it was really not until I reflected upon the scripture as 1st Peter references: *"Your beauty should not come from outward adornment; instead it should be that of your inner self, the unfading beauty of a gentle and quiet spirit, which is of great worth in God's sight."* The meaning of beauty, as it had been infused in my mind, was about being caught up in the appearance of outwardly beauty, in effect, masking the true self. I became aware in recognizing that the image in the mirror was not about seeing the physical being, but rather embracing a spirit of true inner beauty of what God has made. And whatever God has made is in itself a *"wonderfully talented, unique and distinctly beautiful creation."*

True reflection…it is a light of true beauty, for it reflects God's beauty, His loving spirit that shines within.

"I praise You because I am fearfully and wonderfully made;
Your works are wonderful, I know that full well."
Psalm 139:14

A Question *of Beauty!*
It is what it is!!!

A little girl who felt she was not attractive always found herself looking at the outer beauty of others to mimic their appearance. She continually prayed to God that she would become just as pretty as her friends who seemed to attract so many. She prayed always... *"God, please, if you would only give me the beauty that I so desire, it would make me so happy, and I will have many friends and really feel special. Please Lord, she would ask and continually pray."*

Every day, she prayed, the same prayer...and after so long, became frustrated and confused, wondering why her prayer was not being answered.

Her mother saw the dismay on her face and inquired of her, *"child, is there something wrong? It seems you have really been very depressed."*

The little girl said, *"I have been praying and praying every day for God to make me beautiful, just like my friends, but my prayers have not been answered."*

"Mom," she said with sadness in her eyes, *"it seems that when God was passing out blessings of beauty, He must have forgotten about me. My hair does not shine like the light of the wind. I am not eloquently thin, and all that I have ever wanted to do, was to be smart and pretty just like you."*

Upon hearing these words, which were heartbreaking for her mother to hear, she answered in a comforting tone and said to her daughter very firmly, but compassionately...

Listen dear...

*T*he Answer...

Child, don't you know you are already uncompromisingly
beautiful, and abundantly very blessed?...
You were uniquely made by God, and this one thing you must
Remember and never forget.

And because you see others in a different light than yours,
Does not make your light shine any less.

Beauty, my child,
Is just what it is.
No matter how you try to describe it...
Whether light,
Whether dark,
Brown, black,
Yellow, red
Or white.

Beauty is
Just what it is!

No matter
How young or old...
Strong or even
Bold.
The way you walk,
Or the way you talk.
No matter how
Short, thin
Or tall.

Beauty is
Just what it is.

As the colors are to
An alluring light--

So it is to the eloquent winged
Beauty of an illusive
Butterfly in flight.

Each unique and beautiful
In its own right.

Like the Lioness
That prowls
In the midst of the night--
So
Proud
She walks my child…
With her
Head
Held high.

For the beauty of her strength
Availeth much--
In the Pride she savors in
Every strut.

For she walks confidently
And radiates in her stride--
A hidden light that proclaims
Her strength and boldness
Of beauty inside.

Like the gentle flow of
The melting rain,
Cascading down so free…
So is the beauty of its elegance,
Its gentleness, and its powerful surge,

Awaiting to burst into the arms
Of a glistening stream, so anxiously.

Beauty is a shining light that
You see my child is seen by
God, differently than man…

We all are uniquely different,
that's what
sets us all apart.

Man looks at the outward
appearance, but
You see, God looks at the heart.

So when you get down on your
Knees and pray,
Child remember this.
Know that what you ask for,
It already
Exists.

Beauty is
Everything that God has made…
100% natural.
The beauty you crave is hidden inside…
(It's God's light shining through).

And it is certainly true…
Beauty is
Just what it is
My child.

Beauty is…
The essence of You!!!

1 Samuel 16:7
The LORD does not look at the things man looks at. Man looks at the outward appearance, but the LORD looks at the heart.

Psalm 103:1
Bless the Lord, O my soul, and all that is within me, bless his holy name!

Psalm 139:14
I praise you because I am fearfully and wonderfully made; your works are wonderful, I know that full well.

Proverbs 31:30
Charm is deceptive, and beauty is fleeting; but a woman who fears the LORD is to be praised.

Romans 13:14
Rather clothe yourselves with the LORD Jesus Christ, and do not think about how to gratify the desires of the sinful nature.

Colossians 3:12
Therefore as God's chosen people, holy and dearly loved, clothe yourselves with compassion, kindness, gentleness, and patience.

1 Peter 3:4
Instead, it should be that of your inner self, the unfading beauty of a gentle and quiet spirit which is of great worth in God's sight.

Psalm 34:5
Those who look to him are radiant; their faces are never covered with shame.

*S*aints of Praise

A tribute...

*Yet a time is coming and has now come when
the true worshippers will worship the Father in
spirit and truth, for they are the kind of worshippers
the Father seeks. God is spirit and His worshippers
must worship in spirit and in truth.*
                    John 4:23:24

Saints of Praise
A tribute...

Proverbs 31:10
"Who can find a virtuous woman?
For her price is far above rubies."

Proverbs 31:10, offers truly the characteristics of a virtuous woman. Such characteristics as *nobility, wisdom, faithfulness,* and that of being *god-fearing* describe the virtuous woman. This proverb also brings to mind thoughts of someone who was very dear to me, my aunt, Geneva B. Collins. Known as *"Auntie,"* to some and *"Momma Collins"* to others, she through my eyes, exemplified the characteristics of a virtuous woman, and was one truly dedicated to the mission of serving God.

As I reflect on scriptures of *Proverbs 31:10*, I am reminded of many loving acts of kindness of my aunt's life's works and deeds. The passage of *Proverbs 31:16 states: "She considers a field and buys it; out of her earnings she plants a vineyard."* There were times when I watched as she rose from sun up to sun down, working tirelessly in her garden, *"the field of her vineyard."* Her home was always open to others and was very warm and friendly. Often visitors, family and friends would stop by on any occasion, just to partake of the fruits of her labor. She so caringly made sure that upon their visit, they each had their fill of love, good food and conversation. Her arms were always open to everyone in a most kind, unique and loving way.

Proverbs 31:20, states, "she extends her hand to the poor, and she stretches out her hands to the needy." There were also times I can recall watching her ramble around in her purse looking for a little extra change to share with others. She was always willing and ready to give, because that was her nature. It gave her such pleasure to share a little smile of happiness whenever she could.

Although the poetic passage, *Pearls of a Virtuous Woman,* is a tribute to my aunt, it is also in recognition of all the many saints whom I have referenced as *Saints of Praise,* who have a genuine spirit and love of giving true worship and praise to the Lord.

The first of these *Saints of Praise* I refer to as the *"Mother of Pearl Saints."* These are the worshippers that remind me of the *"Mission Mothers,"* who usually sit quaintly on the front pews of the church, and often times during the midst of worship service, proclaim a praise in the lifting of their hands, tapping of their feet, or just sweetly humming a tune of joy in their hearts.

The *"Hidden Pearl Saints"* are often those that are very quiet and shy. My aunt was one of these worshippers. And although these saints may have such a demeanor, they still show however, a spirit of delight in giving a solid, strong, bold, yet gentle praise which radiates a genuine spirit and love of the Lord.

Then there are the *"Shoutin' Halleluiah Pearl Saints,"* which are the saints who usually if no one else is praising, you will most likely find them *singing, dancing, shouting, jumping,* and just having a good time praising and witnessing in the spirit of the Lord, as they very well please.

As the pearl itself symbolizes beauty; its origin, I feel, bears similarities to these *"Saints of Praise."* Each, in their own way is unique and continues to evolve, *becoming in time, solid, refined, resilient, and beautiful precious gems…God's purposeful creations.*

The Pearls of a Virtuous Woman, is truly attributed to all saints and true worshippers, who embody the characteristics and qualities of a virtuous woman.

*"She is a real pearl, a godly woman...
truly a woman of virtue."*

The Pearls of a Virtuous Woman

She sits quietly, with her hands dignified,
Her feet clasped gently in place.

Always a kind, sweet disposition,
Always a smile upon her face.

Godliness is her counsel,
A quiet light is she.

Each word she speaks
Is always spoken,
And uttered in silent dignity.

She opens up her home to those in her village,
The doors of her steps
Are covered in love.

The bell of kindness rings at her table,
Her pearls shine thru
Like radiance from above.

An amazing gem-A lovely surprise,
She is a hidden treasure.

The love of the Lord is her reward,
Truly beyond measure.

She is faithful, kindhearted,
Steadfast and true...

> She is a Mother, a Lady,
> A Hidden Pearl
> Truly a
> Woman of Virtue.

Another pearl that is rooted
And firmly grounded
Through and through
Is a solid gem
A Mother of Pearl
For her benchmark is also
Tried and true.

Always mindful of others,
A true servant is she.

Her virtue is shown
In the love she willingly
Gives unselfishly.

Her daily bread she reads
Continually making
It a guiding lamp.

She nurtures her household in the way of
Knowledge and wisdom--
She fills her chambers with the anointing
Of His presence.

Although the agonizing pain of her trials
Have so often been felt too,
She arises still, with strength
Emerging as a treasure,
Becoming resilient, determined
And strong.

The cloak of strength is her favor
Trust in the Lord, her natural defense
The Armour of truth shields and
Protects her,
From all danger,
Hurt and harm.

She is a Mother of Pearl,
　　　　Her steadfast strength
　　　　Is her due.

She is a strong warrior,
　　　　A lady of wisdom,
　　　　Truly a
　　　　　　　Woman of Virtue.

The "Shoutin" Halleluiah Pearl,
Now, she is a live
Wire indeed.

She jumps, shouts, and runs all
About, having a good time
Praising the Lord in the spirit
As she very well please.

"There is so much to get excited about,"
She proclaims
So vehemently ...

"If you don't feel like praising Him,
I'll praise Him,
Just get up...move over
And get out of my way,
For the Lord's been
Too good to me."

On fire for the Lord,
Not ashamed like David, she gives
Undignified Praise,
With such spirit and intensity.

A toe tapping, hand clapping
Full of the Holy Ghost
　　　　Shoutin, Halleluiah Pearl

Worshiper
she is,
indisputably.

A Virtuous Woman,
Many may try to replicate, duplicate,
Seek her wisdom,
Her tenacity,
But no one can
Proclaim her due.

She holds firmly to her Pearls of Virtuosity…
She is a real pearl,
A godly woman,
Truly
A Woman of
Virtue.

Psalm 19: 8-9
The precepts of the LORD are right, giving joy to the heart. The commands of the LORD are radiant, giving light to the eyes.

Proverbs 31:10-31
A wife of noble character who can find? She is worth far more than rubies. Her husband has full confidence in her and lacks nothing of value. She brings him good, not harm, all the days of her life. She selects wool and flax and works with eager hands. She is like the merchant ships, bringing her food from afar. She gets up while it is still dark; she provides food for her family and portions for her servant girls. She considers a field and buys it; out of her earnings she plants a vineyard. She sets about her work vigorously; her arms are strong for her tasks. She sees that her trading is profitable, and her lamp does not go out at night. In her hand she holds the distaff and grasps the spindle with her fingers. She opens her arms to the poor and extends her hands to the needy. When it snows, she has no fear for her household; for all of them are clothed in scarlet. She makes coverings for her bed; she is clothed in fine linen and purple. Her husband is respected at the city gate, where he takes his seat among the elders of the land. She makes linen garments and sells them, and supplies the merchants with sashes. She is clothed with strength and dignity; she can laugh at the days to come. She speaks with wisdom, and faithful instruction is on her tongue. She watches over the affairs of her household and does not eat the bread of idleness.. Her children arise and call her blessed; her husband also, and he praises her: Many women do noble things, but you surpass them all." Charm is deceptive, and beauty is fleeting; but a woman who fears the LORD is to be praised. Give her the reward she has earned, and let her works bring her praise at the city gate.

Psalm 128:1
Blessed is every one that feareth the Lord, that walketh in his ways.

Psalm 128:3
Thy wife shall be as a fruitful vine by the sides of thine house; thy children like olive plants round about thy table.

An Open Letter
of Thanks

I would like to thank my daughter, Brittany D. Batson for her poem entitled: *Epitome of a Lady*. This poetic passage I feel captures the essence and noble qualities of a virtuous woman.

The poem to follow entitled, *To You Mother*, was written for my mother Jewetta C. Moore, who has always epitomized the characteristics of a god-fearing woman. Her dedication and love of the Lord is unwavering.

Both poems, *Epitome of a Lady and To You Mother* are a tribute to the daughters and mothers who strive to walk daily in His abiding Love.

Thank you "Britt," for allowing God to continue to inspire you as an instrument of praise. Thank you Mom for being a loving mother and a role model of a Virtuous woman.

Love you both!

*"Her very being is precisely
made; a custom fit couture."*

-Brittany D. Batson

Epitome of a Lady

You don't have to know her name to determine her life story. Grace, elegance, beauty, charm all generate her glory. Incredible energy penetrates the earth with each step she takes. Her lush lips keep sealed but yet she speaks volumes through each flutter her eyes make. Be tantalized by one glimpse of her chic allure. Her very being is precisely made; a custom fit couture.

What does she do, who is this doe? Whispers breeze by her ears. To know her is to behold her spirit, for the living God she fears. Worth more than gold, diamonds, crystal, pearls and sapphires to say the least; her wit is more brilliant than these. Her passionate verve outshines the brightest light any gem could ever beam.

Well, where is she from, what is her frame? Why not mention her name? Answers to these could be useful but are irrelevant just the same. True femininity is exuded as she slightly positions her wrist. Her poise is pure like her heart, for there the Almighty God exists. In the midst of a rage lies her pleasant peace. She's the mixing medium of fire and ice. Balancing on the thin line of knowledge and wisdom, her exquisite posture keeps her upright. A refreshing aroma sashays the air when her very presence is near. Neither folly nor faux, her deeds are sincere and her intentions are apparently shear.

If questions still remain regarding who she is or how she came to be, remember you don't need her biography in understanding the epitome of a lady.

-Brittany D. Batson

*"A mother's love is rooted and grounded
and begins at conception."*

To You Mother____

I cannot begin to explain exactly
what you mean to me –
For as long as I can remember,
you have been there
loving, nurturing always wanting
the best for me.

Guiding always with a loving hand,
but, neither letting me stray too far away.
Encouraging me when you saw
I was ready to spread my wings,
even though you wanted me to stay.

Although I ventured
far away sometimes,
you still fervently prayed for
God to protect both day and night.

Only a loving kind mother, could
find it in her heart to give love
and believe in me to do the things
she knew were right.

How deep is a mother's love?
How much love do you
continually give?
For true love cannot be measured -
A mother's love is rooted and
grounded and begins at
conception.

For you carried me, nurtured me,
and even through good times
and bad, still loved me,
giving always true love and
protection.

To You Mother –
Who over the years, have been a friend
and confidant… truly wise.

To You Mother –
Who, though short and sweet, stand
truly tall and solid like a rock in my eyes.

To You Mother –
Who even through life's twists and turns
remind me that God is always in control…
Not to worry, He will make everything
Alright.

To You Mother –
Who is a 'Virtuous Woman,' a gem,
a god-fearing woman, precious
in my sight.

To You Mother –
You are a rare find, truly one of a kind,
loving in all that you do.

To You Mother –
I am so glad that it was
God's plan to bless
my life with a loving
mother like you.

A season to emerge into a brand new you!

A Season
in time...

To everything, there is a season,
      a time to grow, a time to change.

To everything, there is a season,
      nothing remains the same.

A time to sing,
      a time to dance
      a time to have a
      chance.

to spring forth, relish the beauty
      and sweet savor of
      eloquence.

To everything there is a season,
      a time to embrace
      and lift life's hidden veil.

What then awaits...
      what will come forth?
      Ahh...only time
      will tell!

Lift up your head and rejoice
      and let your hearts be free.

Open your eyes to envision,
      a whole new world
      to see.

True beauty soon revealed,
     let the sound of the season
     shed its wondrous splendor.

     Let the writer
     write his song.
     Let the poet
     stroke his pen.
     Let the dancers
     lift their feet,
     joyfully
     and then--

Let the chorus of nature's song
rejoice, in celebration
of a new life soon to begin.

You are a beautiful creature yet undiscovered,
     you possess a virtuous song
     awaiting;
          Listen,
          hear the call.

Embrace life's inner beauty;
     a true beauty hidden within
     us all.

To everything there is a season--
     A time to grow,
     A time to change,
     A time to sing,
     A time to dance,
     A time to play a
     new song…
     And then begin
     Anew.

To everything there is a season,
   a time to joyfully
   emerge…

into a season
   of a brand
      new you.

Isaiah 4:3-18
Forget the former things; do not dwell on the past. See, I am doing a
new thing! Now it springs up; do you not perceive it?

Ecclesiastes 3:11
He has made everything beautiful in its time.

Isaiah 60:21-22
Then will all your people be righteous and they will possess the land
forever. They are the shoot I have planted, the work of my hands, for
the display of my splendor. The least of you will become a thousand,
the smallest a mighty nation. I am the LORD; in its time I will do
this swiftly."

Psalm 18-19
He brought me out into a spacious place; he rescued me because he
delighted in me.

2 Corinthians 9:8
And God is able to make all grace abound to you, so that in all things
at all times, having all that you need, you will abound in every good
work.

Ecclesiastes 3:1
To everything there is a season, and a time to every purpose under
the heaven.

Arise, embrace the spirit and light within you!

ARISE

Take now your visions of secluded dreams--unravel them--
Shake them loose from the shackles that bind them.
Let them arise!

Give light and life to their every potential energy;
every thought, every word, every imagination---and let them
speak with unyielding zeal.

Arise...let your mind be free to rise to catch the breeze
of a mighty rushing wind; to soar with strength on the wings
of an eagle; to enliven the proclamation and acclamation of
undiscovered and unknown territory.

Arise... embrace all that you are, all that you can be--
Let not your fears shake your energy,
or intimidation touch any measure of your potentiality.

Arise...look to the sky, and acknowledge your help from
whence cometh on high, and then...

Arise,
Become!
Arise,
Excel!
Arise,
Proclaim,
Arise,
Embrace the spirit and the light that shines within you.

Proverbs 16:3
Commit your works to the LORD, and your plans will be established.

Psalm 37:5
Commit thy way unto the LORD; trust also in him; and he shall bring it to pass.

Psalm 118: 25
O LORD, save us; O LORD, grant us success.

Isaiah 1:19
If you are willing and obedient, you shall eat the good of the land.

Matthew 6:33
But seek first the kingdom of God and His righteousness, and all these things shall be added to you.

Philippians 4:19
And my God will meet all your needs according to his glorious riches in Christ Jesus.

Psalm 37:4
Delight thyself also in the LORD and he shall give thee the desires of thine heart.

Changes...

- Release the trap—see things differently.
- Explore and imagine the possibilities.
- Reflect a true light, a reflection of God's beauty.
- Believe in yourself to find what truly lies within.
- Arise, embrace the spirit and light *within you.*

Prayer

Oh Lord, we are true vessels that You have made. Each one uniquely
designed and created. Help us to be the light that shines and
reflects the essence of Your beauty shining within.

Amen

Chapter Four
Transformation

And we may grow to emerge in the newness of You.

Transformation

A New Me in You

Identity is the essence of one's thoughts, one's heart,
one's body...the depth and soul of our being.
All that we are is a statement of who we are,
who God made us to be...
It is our Identity.

Doris M. Batson

As I grow continually toward my aspirations to evolve, I am learning the importance of having a willing attitude to extend myself beyond the perimeter and boundaries that were so often set; and which at times, hindered my efforts toward seeking purpose.

Evolving, as I have come to realize, is about finding courage and the wherewithal to step out of boundaries and to explore the potential expectations of our desired aspirations. As *2ndTimothy 1:7 states: "God, has not given us a spirit of timidity, but of courage, of love and of a sound mind."* He enlivens within us a spirit of determination and steadfast patience. Patience in recognizing that as we grow, He will in due time and due season help us to find identity and set us on course to experience new adventures and discoveries in our efforts and pursuit of purpose.

I am reminded of the story of a young sparrow whose desire was to seek discovery in learning how to fly. Everyday, the little sparrow would watch the other hatchlings in the nest spread their wings and fly away. It soon began wondering why it could not fly and soar like the others, and became anxious to fly along with them. The mother bird stayed on her guard, however, to protect the little sparrow from venturing off too soon, as she felt it was not yet nurtured enough and ready to fly on its own.

Each day as the young sparrow tried relentlessly to leave its nest, the mother bird would swoop down immediately to pick her up. However, as her young one continued to grow and after caring and nurturing for it to the best of her ability, she then felt it was time to "to let go" to allow it to find its way to test its wings.

Slowly, as the little bird tried to take flight, each time it would fail. As it tried over and over again to fly, its wings would flutter tirelessly. Later, as the young sparrow tried once again to fly, still struggling for balance in its attempt to flap its wings so freely, it all at once forgot its fright.

"Suddenly the young bird was flying!" It was discovering a whole new world, coming into its own, and doing what it was already preordained to do and to eventually become. "It also let go," so to speak, of its inhibitions and began to allow its natural ability God instinctively gives to overshadow its reluctance.

So, it is in our lives; throughout the *journey of discovery*, God allows us to grow and to be guided and nurtured, and in time, when we are ready, helps us to find our way. As we begin to take off in flight, sometimes in efforts to seek new discoveries and adventures, at times we may incur, *"bumps in the road."* However, as we allow ourselves to *let go and let God,"* we can begin to *"seize the moment"* of our season and forget about our inhibitions in thinking in terms of what we cannot do, and come to an understanding that *with "God, the potential and possibilities are limitless."*

The *journey of evolving* is about believing and trusting that what lies within our spirit is a true destiny of what we may become. It is having faith, patience and determination to be bold enough to take a *"leap of faith,"* but humble enough to allow God to prepare us for the landing. God loves us, and in due season; will assuredly guide us from our *"nest of safety,"* to find purpose and the desires of our hearts, if we allow His spirit to indwell within.

"God is the Identity in my Life."

Identity I

I was conceived, designed, inspired,
    and created by God.

From my mother's womb, I traveled
through the inner chambers of a
spiraling concave, quickening to the
awakening of a moment.
An unforeseen moment, which
propelled my state of being
from darkness into the marvelous
light.

A Creation am I.
One like none other, one of a kind,
Unique,

Why?
Because God created me, That's Why!!!
He knew me full well, even before
I was formed into my state of being.
"My frame was not hidden from you
    when I was made in the secret place.
When I was woven together in the depths
of the earth," Thus saith the Lord.
He knows me,
He knows "when I sit and when I rise."
He knows "my thoughts from near and afar."
He knows my going out and my
coming in, and the words on my
tongue, even before
I speak or utter a word.
      He knows me full well.

A State of being am I!
Why?

Because GOD IS THE STATE OF MY BEING!
That's Why!

Some say a state of being, is the strength of
one's character--
>Like the Lioness that makes her
>presence
>known by the graciousness in her stride.
>I embrace the character of her strength.
>Strong willed, yet determined. Bold,
>yet,
>Humble and proud. Cautious, yet
>vigilant.
>She lives every moment with her eyes
>gazed upon the horizon, with an
>emphatic
>and determined will to survive.
>Strength and character is her Pride!

Why?
>Because she possess the beauty and
>presence of grace and walks proudly,
>and
>fearlessly, with the spirit of
>His light hidden inside.

Imagine this—
>My state of being coinciding with my
>state of mind, where the destiny of
>of pursuit leads me to find, that if I
>believe, God will make all
>things imaginable achievable.

>For A Dreamer am I.

If I can imagine it, I can believe it.
If I can believe it, I can pursue it.
With God, there is nothing
Impossible.

Because He is the destiny of my
Pursuit and purpose.

With God...

There is no mountain unreachable,
No dream unimaginable,
No valley impassible,
No river uncrossible,
No pursuit unconquerable.
Nothing that can
hold me back,
If I believe;
and have faith,
the size of the
grain of a
tiny mustard seed,
I can do anything.

I can, if I believe,
with the wish
of a notion,
take the farthest thoughts
of my intrinsic mind and gather them
with affirmation--Then with
His blessings, proclaim
Jubilant Proclamation.

I can, if I believe,
rise like the breeze of a
dancing wind that
soars so free--

To proclaim my purpose
And identity.

If I believe,
And I do believe,
Because, all that I am is who God
Made me to be.
He is my state of Identity.

And I do believe,
Why?

Because *"I can do all things thru Christ
Who strengthens me."*

Now…stand back
And
Watch me
Fly!!!

Identity II
I Am Woman...

*W*ho am I?

I was conceived, designed, inspired and created by
God.

A creation am I.
One like none other, one of a kind, unique,
Why?

Because God created me,
That's Why...

> From the inner chambers of my mother's
> womb, I traveled through a spiraling concave,
> quickening to the awakening of a moment. An
> unforeseen moment.
> A moment, which propelled my state of being
> from darkness into the marvelous light.

A state of being am I
Why?
> Because God is the state of my being.
> He knows me, and He knew me full well, even
> before I was formed into my being.
> *"My frame was not hidden from you when I was
> made in the secret place...When I was woven
> together in the depths of the earth," thus saith the
> Lord...*
> He knows me full well.

He knows when I sit and when I rise.
He knows my going out and my coming in.
He knows the words on my tongue, even
before
I speak or utter a word.
He knows me and all that I aspire to be.

For a Dreamer am I.
And I realize there is nothing I can't do if I
truly believe.

For with God
If I believe,
There is no door impossible,
No mountain unreachable
No valley impassible,
No river uncrossible,
No dream unimaginable,
No pursuit unconquerable,
To hold me back.

If I believe,
I can rise on the reveling wings of an eagle.

If I believe,
I can run and not grow weary, walk and not
faint.

If I believe,
I can, on the breeze of a dancing wind,
soar to heights so free,
If I believe.

And I do believe
Because God is all that is within me.
He is my identity.

Who am I?
A wife, A mother,
A sister, A woman,
A friend,
and this I can't deny.
But most of all
A child of God am I,
And I truly believe
"I can do all things thru Christ who strengthens
me,"
Now stand back,
     And
     watch me
     Fly!!!

Psalm 31:5
Into your hands I commit my spirit; redeem me, O LORD, the God of truth.

Psalm 18:31-36
For who is God besides the LORD? And who is the Rock except our God? It is God who arms me with strength and makes my way perfect. He makes my feet like the feet of a deer; he enables me to stand on the heights. He trains my hands for battle; my arms can bend a bow of bronze. You give me your shield of victory, and your right hand sustains me; you stoop down to make me great, You broaden the path beneath me, so that my ankles do not turn.

Psalm 71:6
From birth I have relied on you; you brought me forth from my mother's womb. I will ever praise you.

Job 33:4
The Spirit of God has made me; the breath of the Almighty gives me life.

2 Corinthians 9:8
And God is able to make all grace abound to you, so that in all things at all times having all that you need, you will abound in every good work.

Psalm 139:14-16
I praise you because I am fearfully and wonderfully made; your works are wonderful, I know that full well. My frame was not hidden from you when I was made in the secret place. When I was woven together in the depths of the earth. Your eyes saw my unformed body. All the days ordained for me were written in your book before one of them came to be.

A Change…
A New Me in You!!!

A metamorphosis, a transformation,
An amazing creation of beauty…
Set free…

Metamorphosis

A butterfly in motion
A beautiful sight to see.

A creation born to be transformed
into an emergence of change
A metamorphosis set free.

A tiny seed conceived
A new life soon to begin--

To reveal an enlivened spirit
Of grace and beauty, amazingly
Transforming from within.

Nourished daily,
Shielded with abundance and care;

Even though helpless and alone
In every situation,
His loving presence is always there.

Like the fervor of the mighty rushing wind
A new life emerges miraculously...

A metamorphosis, a transformation,
An amazing creation of beauty
Set free.

Like the seasons that change,
One day, I too will gain,
A newness of life to begin.

Like the seasons that change
No longer the same
An enigma of beauty transformed
From within.

A change will come
One day in time,
And as I grow
And am strengthened by His grace,
Please, just be patient with me.

A metamorphosis, a change,
New life, I too will gain,
To one day become, what God
Purposefully and
Truly wants me to be!

Romans 12:2
Do not conform any longer to the pattern of this world, but be transformed by the renewing of your mind. Then you will be able to test and approve what God's will is—his good, pleasing and perfect will.

2 Corinthians 5:17
Therefore, if anyone is in Christ, he is a new creation; the old has gone, the new has come!

Isaiah 40:31
But those who hope in the LORD will renew their strength. They will soar on wings like eagles; they will run and not grow weary, they will walk and not be faint.

Lamentations 3:22-23
Because of the LORD's great love we are not consumed, for his compassions never fail. They are new every morning; great is your faithfulness.

2 Corinthians 3:17-18
Now the LORD is the Spirit, and where the Spirit of the LORD is, there is freedom. And we, who with unveiled faces all reflect the LORD's glory, are being transformed into his likeness with ever-increasing glory, which comes from the LORD, who is the Spirit.

*"Open your eyes, to receive the beauty
and delight of God's hidden surprise!"*

Becoming

There is a sweet fragrance, in the air
The joy of spring has arrived.

Lift up your head, give rise to His goodness.
Behold the beauty and delight of
God's hidden surprise.

In the fields loom the roses, and shower of
flowers
growing wild and free.

Over the mountains,
the beasts of the field, the lions, the goats,
the horses, and the sheep all awaken
from their slumber
so comfortably.

In the midst of the breeze emerge the trees,
spreading their limbs
rising fluently in the air.

All Becoming, awakening,
yielding the fruits of their labor,
soon to bear.

The stars, awaken,
and light up the heavens
rejoicing delightfully in song.

Like the sun and the moon,
they too are becoming
all in due season—
to each its own.

All creatures, all things
Awakening- becoming
now blissfully in full view.

And like the embrace of a new day dawning...
I arise...
to claim my change..

For I too,
am becoming.

Colossians 3:10
And have put on the new self, which is being renewed in knowledge in the image of its Creator.

Romans 12:2
Do not conform any longer to the pattern of this world, but be transformed by the renewing of your mind. Then you will be able to test and approve what God's will is—his good, pleasing and perfect will.

2 Peter 3:18
But grow in the grace and knowledge of our Lord and Savior Jesus Christ. To him be glory both now and forever! Amen.

2 Timothy 1:6-7
For this reason I remind you to fan into flame the gift of God, which in you through the laying on of my hands. For God did not give us a spirit of timidity, but a spirit of power, of love and of self-discipline.

Psalm 119:96
To all perfection I see a limit; but your commands are boundless.

1 Chronicles 16:31-34
Let the heavens be glad, and let the earth rejoice: and let men say among the nations, The LORD reigneth. Let the sea roar, and the fullness thereof: let the fields rejoice, and all that is therein. Then shall the trees of the wood sing out at the presence of the LORD, because he cometh to judge the earth. O give thanks unto the LORD; for he is good; for his mercy endureth for ever.

"Oh Yes! I know I am truly and richly blessed!"

*F*abulously & *Richly Blessed*

I can't tell it… Just can't tell it all! How good the Lord has been to me. When I look around and think of all His goodness, I can't help but to praise Him, cause He keeps right on blessing me over and over continuously.

Oh Yes! And I know I'm Blessed!!! I was conceived, designed, by His infinite wisdom and imagination so abundantly. Every inch, every diameter, every tangible vein, was I made; No duplication! No imitation! No replication, He created me, specifically, purposefully and individually. He created the lifeblood and spirit within me!!!

Oh Yes, Yes! And I know I'm blessed!!! I was born into a family of inheritance of the blessed seed of Abraham. And I am thankful, so thankful to be a blessed child, a creation of the Most High and Almighty God, My Father, The Great I AM!!!

Oh Yes! Yes! And I know I'm blessed!!! Because I have found none other who cares for me unconditionally. There is none like Him, None like Him you see. As a matter of fact, My God is the best thing that has ever happened to me!

And Yes! Oh Yes! I know I am truly and richly blessed. Blessed just to Know Him…to Reverence Him, to Give Him Honor, Thanks and the Glory. For in Him, I find, complete love, peace, happiness, and all the rest…

And if you seek these things, you can have it, just let me suggest…Get to know Him…My God, My Father, My Savior, My Creator, My Everything. Get to know Him, and you too can become wondrously,

Fabulously and richly blessed.

Psalm 25:13
He will spend his days in prosperity, and his descendants will inherit the land.

Psalm 145:16
You open your hand and satisfy the desires of every living thing.

Philippians 4:19
But my God shall supply all your need according to his riches in glory by Christ Jesus.

Colossians 1:27
To them God has chosen to make known among the Gentiles the glorious riches of this mystery, which is Christ in you, the hope of glory.

Psalm 16:6
The boundary lines have fallen for me in pleasant places; surely I have a delightful inheritance.

Isaiah 44:3-4
For I will pour water on the thirsty land, and streams on the dry ground; I will pour out my spirit on your offspring, and my blessing on your descendants, they will spring up like grass in a meadow, like poplar trees by flowing streams.

Galatians 3:29
If you belong to Christ, then you are Abraham's seed, and heirs according to the promise.

Press on in pursuit of a journey…Press on anyhow!

*P*ersistence,
Press On!

I've Pressed my way through valleys of oppression--
it seems so many --

I've Pressed my way through the storms of life and of
those, I've had plenty --

I've Pressed my way when the light was dim, and
couldn't seem to find my way through the shadows
that stalked my fear --

I Pressed on, Persistent - knowing the light of His
love dwells within and is there to always guide--in
every situation, He is there --

Though provoking circumstances sought the conquest
of my soul, and despite endless attempts sometimes
to abuse and scandalize my name--

I Pressed on, because I was fearfully and wonderfully
made, to stand firm and not clammer under pressure,
for *"that is why for Christ's sake, I delight in weaknesses,
in insults, in hardships, in persecutions, in difficulties, for
when I am weak, then I am strong,"* for only victory in
His Name do I claim --

With the weight of futility wrenching heavily against
my brow, and yet, when others still don't seem to
quite understand —

> I Press on -
> > in pursuit of a journey
> I Press on -

with an enlivened spirit
I Press on –
with persistence,
fortitude and gratitude
I Press on -
For I know
who holds my hand.

To a friend and fellow poet,
Tricia Billington…
"Keep the Faith." Press On!

2 Corinthians 4:8-9
We are hard pressed on every side, but not crushed; perplexed, but not in despair, persecuted, but not abandoned; struck down, but not destroyed.

2 Corinthians 12:10
That is why, for Christ's sake, I delight in weaknesses, in insults, in hardships, in persecutions, in difficulties. For when I am weak then I am strong.

2 Timothy 1:7
For God did not give us a spirit of timidity, but a spirit of power, of love and of self-discipline.

2 Timothy 2:3
Endure hardship with us like a good soldier of Christ Jesus.

Ephesians 6:9
And let us not be weary in well doing: for in due season we shall reap, if we faint not.

1 Corinthians 15:58
Therefore, my beloved brethren, be steadfast, immovable, always abounding in the work of the Lord, knowing that your labor is not in vain in the Lord.

Philippians 3:12
Not that I have already obtained all this, or have already been made perfect, but I press on to take hold of that for which Christ Jesus took hold of me.

James 1:2-4
Consider it pure joy, my brothers, whenever you face trials of many kinds, because you know that the testing of your faith develops perseverance. Perseverance must finish its work so that you may be mature and complete, not lacking anything.

Seize the moment-for its time to shine!

It's Time
to Shine!!!

Light up the moment,
It's a brand new day--
Greet the possibilities,
That comes your way.

Get ready...get moving,
It's time to take your place.
Imagine it... claim it,
The endless possibilities await.

Hope is yours...take note of it,
And take life's open door--
To take the time, to leave
behind, whatever was
holding you back before.

Your greatness is measured
In the spirit of you —
what you think--what you
believe and certainly
What you can pursue.

It's your time...your moment,
Now grab hold,
Don't let go--
Seize the moment,
With a new attitude in mind.

Seize the moment,
In a new light,
A new life,
For it's a new day--
And it's time, to
Shine!

Psalm 34:5
Those who look to him are radiant; their faces are never covered with shame.

Psalm 89:15
Blessed are those who have learned to acclaim you, who walk in the light of your presence, O LORD.

Proverbs 4:18
The path of the righteous is like the first gleam of dawn, shining ever brighter till the full light of day.

1ˢᵗ Peter 2:9-10
But you are a chosen people, a royal priesthood, a holy nation, a people belonging to God, that you may declare the praises of him who called you out of darkness into his wonderful light.

Luke 8:16
No one lights a lamp and hides it in a jar or puts it under a bed. Instead, he puts it on a stand so that those who come in can see the light.

John 1:1-4
In the beginning was the Word, and the Word was with God, and the Word was God. He was with God in the beginning. Through him all things were made; without him nothing was made that has been made. In him was life, and that life was the light of men.

Metamorphosis, a transformation-
an amazing creation of beauty set free...

- *The virtuous woman, a godly woman, truly a woman of virtue.*
- *A creation am I...one of a kind...unique, why?*
  Because God created me, that's why!
- *It's a new light, new life, new day-seize the moment—*
  it's time to shine!

Purposefully

For whatever reason,
God placed me
here on this earth

Of His will and creation,
I was given birth

For whatever reason,
He took me and
Shaped me by His
Almighty Hands,
and fashioned and
sculpted me
In the image
of His own

He gave me Life,
And my life
became His,
and
His alone

For whatever reason,
God preconceived
and looked upon me,
so caringly, like the
stars, the sun,
the moon and the
light of the heavens
that shine
above

For whatever reason
God chose me,
To be His creation
To cherish and to
Love

For whatever reason,
Only God knows,
Of this I am sure
But I am so glad
that He
thought of me
Created and
ordained me

For whatever reason
to become His
intended purpose
Purposefully

Jeremiah 29:11-13

For I know the plans I have for you, declares the LORD, plans to prosper you and not to harm you, plans to give you hope and a future. Then you will call upon me and come and pray to me, and I will listen to you. You will seek me and find me when you seek me with all your heart.

Prayer

*Lord, we thank You, for the bountiful blessings You have given us.
We pray that You will allow us to become aware of our potential
and that we
may come to know purpose for our lives according to Your Will.
We ask and Pray in Your Holy and Righteous Name.*

Amen

Appendix

This self-discovery guide is a study reference for spiritual growth and enrichment toward finding a renewal and awareness of self-discovery. Its purpose is to provide a personal insight into revealing possible strengths that may be hidden and to bring these strengths to the forefront.

As you examine and take part in this study reference guide, it is my prayer that you become more and more spiritually blessed. Seek Him first and be assured in knowing, God has a plan and purpose for you. He will in due time lead and guide you toward discovering your path...potential and a purposeful life.

Evolving
Reference & Study Guide

This self-discovery study guide references four areas of study: Seek, Trust, Believe, and Pursue. These areas will hopefully inspire enlightenment and affirmation toward spiritual growth and renewal.

As you begin your study growth program, reflect upon scriptural references and record daily personal goals and achievements.

Think on these things:

1. *Are you still holding on to the reigns in your life trying to control your own path? If so, what areas are you finding yourself still attempting to control?*

2. *Are you seeking a breakthrough in your life? What must you do to prepare yourself?*

3. *What are your interests?*

4. *Have you ever been encouraged or complimented regarding your talents?*

5. *Are you open minded and open to change? Are you accustomed to doing things in a routine manner?*

6. *Do you find yourself imitating others; or, are you your own person?*

Seek (meditate and reflect)

Matthew 6:33: "But seek ye first the kingdom of God, and His righteousness, and all these things shall be added unto you."

Reflection inspires contemplation and time to search within...time to open our hearts and minds to embrace potentially new ideas and discoveries. It is important to reflect upon where we have been and to ask ourselves what we aspire to accomplish in life?

Write on the following:

1. *Accomplishments you have made both past and present.*

2. *Hidden weaknesses that may be a stronghold.*

3. *Talents or strengths.*

4. *Things you may have tried to accomplish in regards to your intended purpose.*

Meditate:
> *Scripture references: Isaiah 4:3-18   Ecclesiastes 3:11*
> *2 Corinthians 9:8*
> *Chapter Three: Changes, True Reflections*

*Daily Prayer:*_____

_____

_____

_____

_____

_____

Enlightenment (taking time to listen)

Proverbs 3:5-6 states: *"Trust in the LORD with all your heart and lean not on your own understanding; in all your ways acknowledge him, and he will make your paths straight."*

Have you ever been encouraged or complimented regarding your talents? If so, did you take the comment lightly or for granted, thinking of it perhaps as just a nice or polite gesture?

From time to time without knowledge or forethought, words to inspire our spirit may be enlivened upon us. God speaks to us in many ways. And we should be mindful to take time to listen; realizing such inspiration may be placed upon our spirit to initially uplift, intrigue and stir our imagination. Eternalize the inspiration and believe with assurance, God will in time reveal the path of a purposeful and fulfilling life.

Write on the following:

1. List compliments or comments, spoken kindly of you.

2. Make a list of your hobbies or interests.

_____
_____
_____

3. Which of these hobbies or interests gives you most a feeling of self-fulfillment?
   Write how you may have felt or feel when you share your hobby or interest with others.

Meditate:

Scripture references: Psalm 29:3-4   Job 26:14
Lamentations 3:26   John 10:3-4
Chapter Two: The Spirit of Humility. Poems: Embrace,
Whisper, Touched by the Potter's Hand

Daily Prayer:_____

_____

_____

_____

_____

_____

Believe (renewal of new discoveries, new insights)

Romans 12:2 states: "Do not conform any longer to the pattern of this world, but be transformed by the renewing of your mind. Then you will be able to test and approve what God's will is—his good, pleasing and perfect will."

Are you willing to become open to change? Change takes patience and courage to do and see things in a different way. As you seek to grow and evolve, seek renewal of strength in the renewing of your mind and spirit to enliven your aspirations of purpose.

Write at least ten positive motivating words that describes your strengths.

1._____   6._____
2._____   7._____
3._____   8._____
4._____   9._____
5._____   10._____

- *Make a list of things you desire to accomplish and to change, which you feel may help you to continue to grow.*

- *Write at least 10 or more positive motivational words that could inspire your belief and potential to succeed.*

- *Prayer and Share with others for strength and spiritual growth. (Exchange positive strengths of each other).*

Meditate:

*Scripture references: Psalm 42:5 John 16:24 Isaiah 40:31
Hosea 10:12 Isaiah 43:18-19   2 Corinthians 5:17
2 Corinthians 3:17-18 Romans 12:2
Poems: Identity II, A Season in Time, Metamorphosis*

Daily Prayer:_____

_____

_____

_____

_____

_____

Perseverance (persist & pursue your dreams)

Philippians 2:13 states: "For it is God who works in you to will and to act according to His good purpose."

In reference to having persistence and determination to realize fulfilling purpose in our lives, I am reminded of Paul's reference in 2 Corinthians 4:8-9 which states: "We are hard pressed on every side, but not crushed; perplexed, but not in despair; persecuted, but not abandoned; struck down, but not destroyed." Be courageous and strong in the Lord, for as Romans 8:37 states: "know, in all these things we are more than conquerors through him who loved us."

Stay in Pursuit of your dreams, ideas, and convictions. You'll find that the dream of your pursuit is within reach, with God leading the way.

Write an Affirmation statement of your desire of Purpose:

_____

_____

_____

_____

_____

Meditate:

Scripture references: 2 Corinthians 4:8-9 2 Corinthians 12:10 2 Thessalonians 1:11 Philippians 4:19 Philippians 3:12 James 1:2-4 Psalm 119:96 Poems: Persistence, Press On, It's Time to Shine, Purposefully

Daily Prayer:_____

_____

_____

_____

_____

_____

Notes

About the Author

Writing "poetry of inspiration" to inspire the soul is the passion of Doris M. Batson. Her work speaks with a voice that offers hope to never give up on the pursuit of a dream. Aside from writing, she is a teacher, musician and artist. Among one of her books is one co-written along with her father, Rev. P.R. Moore entitled: "Restore the Joy," A collection of inspirational poems and prayers. She has a daughter, Brittany D. Batson and currently resides in her hometown of Tyler, Texas. Through the journey of Evolving, Doris shares a personal journey in the search and pursuit of purpose. Each poetic passage inspires a heartfelt message to be encouraged to persist with faith and determination in efforts of seeking fulfilling purpose.

Other Published Work
"RESTORE THE JOY"

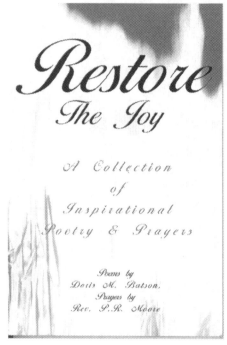

A Collection of Inspirational Poetry and
Prayers by
Doris M. Batson
&
Rev. P.R. Moore

We would love to hear from you.
Contact us at: dmbleo@yahoo.com

Thank you for your support of this book.